Contents

Cover image: photograph taken by Dori (http://commons.wikimedia.org/wiki/User:Dori)

Introduction

If you ask 20 people how to raise horses for fun and profit, you will get 23 opinions. I am going to give you my opinions gathered from years of caring for, showing and breeding horses, as well as dealing with stud farms and trainers. This a practical approach that you will not likely find on the Internet or in a book. I will give you ideas that involve regenerative natural agriculture to make your horses healthier, your work less taxing, your feed bills cheaper and your supplement expenses next to nothing.

My wife and I have had horses for more than 30 years. We are no longer actively showing, but we still have two horses and one donkey. My motto is "Healthy Soil = Healthy Plants and Animals = Healthy People." In other words, if the soil is healthy for *people*, it will be healthy for *horses*.

There is a joke about being in the horse business: How do you make a million dollars in the horse business? Start out with two million.

Owning, training, breeding and caring for horses is a wonderful experience. No matter what the breed, these animals are magnificent, and can give you a lot of joy; however, if you do the things I suggest, you don't have to lose your shirt, and you will meet great people, make great friends — *and* enjoy your horse friends.

There are many considerations before and after you get horses. We cover everything from A to Z that you need to know to be in the horse business. The information will also apply to anyone who just wants a horse as a friend or pet.

You'll learn about:

- The best type of land for raising horses

- What type of water source is the best

- Why you shouldn't use barbed wire fencing

- Do horses really like a barn?

- Some of the best breeds of horses

- Grass fed versus grain fed

- Making sure your soils are in tip-top shape

- Do you really need a tractor?

- The financial concerns of raising horses

Land

1. What kind of land do you have, and/or what can you afford? Generally, you need two to three acres per horse, depending on where you live. I know there are thousands of horses living in small lots without grass all over the world, and I am not suggesting that there is something wrong with this approach, but I would not do it that way.

2. What does the land look like? Trees, brush, grass, hilly, flat but rough? If you don't have a barn, you need a lean-to for the animals to get out of the weather. Brush and/or valleys are fine (to block wind). You need to plan for shelter, grass and other necessities before you clear everything off the land.

3. If you have new land, do you need a bulldozer to level ground, clear fence line or build a pond? They are easy to drive, not too expensive to rent — and a lot of fun to operate!

4. Pasture and hay are important considerations. The farmland in this country was farmed (worn out); trace minerals were removed and the humus depleted more than one hundred years ago.

Fencing

What type of fence do you have? Is it in good condition or bad? Horses require the best you can provide, and barbed wire is a terrible choice. If a horse runs into barbed wire, the cuts can be horrific, and the healing time is long.

1. High tensile electric fence is my favorite. It has stood the test of time as being safe. It keeps horses in, usually keeps predators out and certainly keeps the neighbors' cows or horses at home. It is very inexpensive compared to other kinds of fencing. And electric fencing is a psychological barrier.

2. Woven wire is a good fence but harder to put up and expensive. It will keep horses from sticking their heads through the fence to get outside grass.

3. In my opinion, barbed wire is the worst. It doesn't keep small animals in if they take a notion to get out. Also, when you go down a highway and you see fence bent over, it is because cows and/or horses have put their heads through the fence to eat the grass on the outside. They do this for two reasons:

    *   Not enough grass in their pasture.

    *   The grass on the outside is better quality than on the inside their pasture [more on this later].

4. Wood fence looks good, but the expense and maintenance are heavy. Also, dogs or predators have an open door, so to speak.

5. If you have a basically intact barbed wire fence, you can buy offset attachments to put high tensile wire on the offsets and then hook up a charger.

6. If you fence has "T" post, you need to put plastic caps on the top so a horse cannot come down on the post and impale itself (a horrible accident that is easy to prevent).

7. Chargers come in many sizes and features. The biggest influence is the length of fence and the number of wires you want to charge.

8. Horse electric fence needs to be tall so the horses can't jump over or lean over the top wire.

9. I don't recommend off brand electric chargers. Durability and quality of charge are most important. Two of the best are Primer and Gallagher. We have had electric fence for 26 years, and our first charger lasted 22 years.

10. Gates are also important. I buy 12-foot wide gates for most uses, as a truck, truck and trailer, or tractor can readily go through this width. Occasionally, if you need more width, you can use two 12-foot gates, two 10-foot gates or other combinations. You can buy 16-foot gates, but they get heavy, and you need a special support from which to swing the gate to prevent from sagging.

11. Corner posts are essential, and installation cost is whatever you are willing to pay for: money or backbreaking labor.

12. We have a special device that can be attached to our tractor that drives posts into the ground. With moist soil, you can drive an eight-foot post three feet into the ground in one to three minutes, and they will not lean or come out after you build the "H" braces. These work for electric, stretched woven wire or barbed w ire.

13. You can dig and then put concrete around posts, but this is hard work, and the posts tend to pull out if there is too much tension on the fence wires.

14. I found a new fence system called "The Mule," where you twist an auger into the ground and then attach special fiberglass posts, with one vertical and two at an angle. It is flimsy until the last angled post is attached and then it is almost impossible to pull out of the ground — even with a team of mules or tractor. Effort is low and durability is fantastic. (See the Resources section.)

Water

You have your fence up, and you are ready for the next step, but you don't have any horses — yet. What are you going to do for water? Do you have a pond? A flowing creek? Community water? A water well?

1. Water is essential in a stall or small enclosure. One of the worst things that can happen to a horse is dehydration, and if it is a hot summer day it is even worse. Leave more water than your horse can consume. We found that two 10-gallon buckets was the minimum requirement for a 24 hour period (we still checked it twice a day).

2. What are your water resources for your pasture? Do you have a well, community water, pond or creek, or will you have to haul water? I like automatic float valves for community or well water.

3. What are you going to put the water in? Metal or plastic, short or tall, auto float or hand fill? We prefer metal stock tanks because they usually outlast plastic (I just discovered premade concrete tanks that have the plumbing coming into the bottom, which almost ensures no freezing in the winter). Standard size is fine for horses unless you have miniatures and then they need to be about 12 to 18 inches high.

4. Are you going to live on the farm or commute from a nearby town? You must check your horses at least once a day if you don't live on the farm. You have to check their water. Auto floats are great but not perfect.

5. What are your winters like? Will water troughs freeze? Can you install a heater with electricity or will you want to break ice several times a day (smaller troughs freeze a lot quicker than big ones). If you don't live on the land, the water will need to be broken at least twice a day. The farther north you live, you will need to break ice more frequently.

6. My favorite is a well, if you have good water and enough of it not to go dry. It should be checked to see if it is safe. If it is not safe for people, it isn't healthy for animals. Herbicides, pesticides and heavy metals are toxic to animals.

7. Ponds are great if they are big enough and can survive a drought, but I don't like horses walking in the water or on the sides, because they will destroy your pond. I prefer fencing them off to let weeds and/or grasses grow up to protect against erosion. Also, with plant growth, the water is cleaned and filtered for better health, and you develop a small ecosystem for wildlife (birds, rabbits, etc.)

   When you a healthy pond, you can pump water out into a stock tank inexpensively with no water wasted.

8. A flowing creek is good but not common today unless you live in mountainous areas in the Eastern United States.

9. Community water is most common. It is easy and inexpensive to run water lines to pastures from a central location. You can rent a Ditch Witch® trencher and run plastic PVC pipe and use float valves to control water volume when you are at work or away from home.

   In the beginning, you can use garden hose, but you must have containers that hold enough water so the horses will not run out, and/or you must be available to fill the containers frequently (very unhandy.)

   Garden hose cannot be attached to float valves, because the pressure will make the hose blow up. I use hydraulic hoses and put metal fittings on the ends. They take pressure, last for years and do not freeze easily and break in the winter.

Shelter

1. If you can only do a lot or a stall, then do it well. Well means exercising your horse every day. Do not lock them up and forget them. How would you like being locked in your bedroom and not let out for weeks on end?

2. One of the fundamental things you must do with horses that are confined is get used to the handle of a manure rake. They make a lot of manure and are incapable of cleaning up their own "stuff."

3. If you have access to pasture, your horse will love it, and it is very good for their mental health. Horses are herd animals, and they like to roam, even if it is only from the front of the field to the back.

4. Speaking of herds, horses need buddies, even if it is in the next stall. This is another reason that if you have a single horse, you need to spend time with him or her daily.

5. I will go into pasture health and renovation later, but don't use commercial fertilizers. The chemicals can be toxic.

6. Stalls need some kind of bedding: straw (hard to clean out), wood shavings or rice or peanut hulls (the most common. the best and the easiest to work with).

7. For mares that have babies, it is best to use straw, because it is less dusty than other bedding.

8. Shelter is a consideration, but I am mostly into Mother Nature. Years ago, we built a barn with runs for our horses to get in out of inclement weather. When it rained, they were under the trees and not in the barn. The worst was when it was freezing rain with snow. They had icicles hanging all over their bodies, and they only came in to eat and then went right back outside. Animals want to be in nature, not in a building. They do not have human values or inclinations. Unless you have a show animal or a sick animal, I would leave them outside at all times. There are millions of horses that survive winters in North Dakota and other Northern states with nothing but trees or draws to get out of the wind.

My goal is to make sure they have healthy food and water and they will do fine.

9. Horses stay healthier in the open than when they are confined. Fresh water, fresh air, good grass and/or hay, and some trees for wind shelter and they are fine. If you want disease in your horse herd, confine them like they are in feed lots (or in jail).

10. The exception to letting your horses run is if you don't have the space or if you are showing your horses. It is still important to get them out to stretch by themselves, or you can ride or use a lunge line (more on this later).

Feeding

1. Feeding is also a consideration. We use bunk feeders with a hay rack that we buy from the feed store. These average four to eight feet long, and they hold up for years.

2. If your horse is not in a pasture, he or she will be eating while you are not at home. We checked the stalls morning and evening, added water and hay in the morning and changed the water and gave more hay in the evening. I am mentioning water again, because a horse needs water while eating just as we need water, particularly when eating something dry. Colic is common when there isn't enough water.

3. We also keep minerals in the stall or pasture. Most of the minerals you buy from your feed store are useless. Poor quality salt is almost as bad as no salt.

4. My favorite salt comes from Utah, and it is loaded with trace minerals. The square white, yellow or brownish blocks are are terrible. These companies take salt and remove all the trace minerals and sell them to other industries. They then make white salt, which has no trace minerals. Yellow salt contains sulfur (I haven't figured out its purpose). And, finally, they put about five trace minerals in the salt, and it is brownish red. This is nothing compared to the 70+ trace minerals from a natural source like Redmond.

5. Grains are given to horses to make them fat and give them more energy when working them. They need very little grain when in a pasture environment with little exercise. Many types of grain are used, but, for the most part, they use the cheapest available on the day they bag the product. It has been rumored that food manufacturers put chemicals in the mix to make the horse like their particular product (sort of addicting the animal to XYZ feed). Almost all companies use liquid molasses to mask the taste of cheaper, poor tasting grain and to hide the dust and dirt in the feed. This has been true for years, but now

they use molasses to cover up the taste of genetically engineered organisms (GEOs), particularly soy beans, corn and cotton seed.

6. There have been studies where they take GMO corn and put it in a bunker beside a trough that had regular corn. Cows did not eat the GMO feed until they were starving. They also noticed that squirrels and rats would not eat the GMO corn. If a cow, a rat and a squirrel will not eat GMO corn, why should you feed this to your horses, to yourself or to your family? This stuff is unhealthy for man or beast. We care too much for ourselves and our animals to feed these "Franken Foods."

7. We fortunately live in an area where we have a local mill that makes organic, healthful food for horses, dogs and cats. The owner has a network of farmers that grow non-GMO grains, and he monitors their crops.

8. Winter pastures can use wheat, Elbon rye or annual rye, but they are different. Elbon and wheat have about the same size seed and can go out at the same time, if you want to mix them. They are a lot cheaper per 50 lb bag, but you have to put out three times more, so the cost is moot. To put them out, you must prepare a seed bed, and they need to be drilled into the soil for the best results. You can get a decent stand if you have the prepared seed bed and then drag into the bed with a flexible harrow.

9. On the other hand, you can get a respectable stand with annual rye by broadcasting and dragging it with something to get on the soil beneath the grass. Also, depending on the brand, it will re-seed each year and keep coming back year after year. I didn't like TAM 90 (poor stand). Oregon rye and Gulf Coast rye are okay, but my favorite is Marshall rye grass, which has made the best stand and returns well each year. I also recommend some clover. Some people will get all worked up and tell you that clover will make your horses sick. But horses really don't like clover, and I only use a small amount to help the soil. I have never tried a clover that stands up, and that could be different in terms of horses eating it. I use white clover that has runners. We have been raising horses since 1977 and never had a problem with clover.

10. If you live in the South, fire ants can be a problem. These are nasty little critters with a painful bite. All kinds of chemicals are used; however, besides these chemicals being toxic to people and the environment, they only move the ants to new location. The ants will return in six months. Organic or natural is the best way to eliminate ants. We use a combination of products. In a five-gallon bucket mix 1 ounce of orange oil (a great natural cleaning product), 1 cup of liquid

molasses, 1 cup of compost tea, and 2 ounces of diatomacous earth. Stir well and pour all five gallons down the center of the mound. This may need to be repeated one more time depending on the size and depth of the mound. I have also discovered that Splenda® and Equal® mixed together will kill the ants.

11. I am opposed to supplements for people or horses, or for whatever, because we should be getting what we need from the soil. This is particularly true for horses; however, the correct things are not in the soil—not yet. In the meantime, my favorite supplement for animals is humates. Humates are made up of humic acids, fulvic acids and chelated trace minerals. The humic and fulvic acids help to detoxify the chemicals that animals get from the soil and hay.

12. The chelated trace minerals are life-giving nutrients that let the body work properly. Our bodies—humans, cows, horses, dogs, and animals of all kinds—need quality trace minerals so our chemical factory functions properly. The best humates come from a company in New Mexico (http://www.humates.com/), and they are the most knowledgeable in the field. Humates have been used to detoxify toxic waste sites and chemical spills, besides the benefits to animals and people.

13. Management intensive grazing (MIG) has to do with dividing your land into little sections by using portable electric fence. You move the horses to a new section (can be divided into two acres, five acres or some percentage of your total pasture land). This technique makes the horses eat all the grass, including the less desirable grass. This lets the cell rest for about 28 days, allowing the grass to recover and growing more grass in the future.

14. One more comment about killing fire ants. I have found that you can use Equal (aspartame) or Splenda (sucrolose) on fire ant mounds. If you put enough on the mound, and water it in with enough water (about 10 gallons), you will destroy the mound. Splenda is a chlorinated hydrocarbon. It is in the same family as DDT, which is the pesticide that almost wiped out the Bald Eagle.

Horse Breeds

1. What type of horses do you want?

   Do you want performance horses, halter horses or pleasure? Which breed?

2. My wife and I decided that we liked Arabian horses. I believed they were exceptional athletes, and I set out to prove it. I was able to prove that the right Arabian could hold his own with Quarter Horses in reining classes, but what I proved didn't pay off in dollars. More on this later. There are many breeds and they all have a place for your pleasure. A grade horse can be fine also for performance and pleasure. Sometimes, a cross of two purebreds makes an outstanding mount (½ Arab and ½ Quarter Horse is outstanding). When deciding, look at every combination or breed and decide what you want to do. But watch out for hype from breeders and horse traders.

3. There are all kinds of events for horses, for all ages, and for professional riders and amateur riders. A professional rider/trainer makes his or her living training, showing and/or teaching about horses. An amateur is someone who rides for fun without getting paid. There are two types of amateurs. One is the person who is as good as a professional but doesn't want to change status, and the second is the beginner to intermediate. When you start out, the second category is where you begin. All breeds make many levels or divisions, so beginners can start and get experience without being blown away by more experienced competitors.

4. You also need to find someone to help you. Some breeders and trainers are very honest and helpful. This is sort of "buyer beware," but you must search for the honest one to minimize your mistakes. When you find the right people, they will guide you in the selection of your first horse or horses. They are not all dishonest, but you have to have help. Some sellers will drug their wild horses, and they will be great in the sale ring, only to be crazy and unmanageable when you get them home. For this reason, it is best to visit a potential horse and seller several times before you make your purchase, and "pop in" unannounced at least once.

Horsemanship

1. One of my pet peeves is parents buying a horse for their child and then letting the child go down the highway right-of-way with no training, risking the child's life. The proper way is to buy a 100% safe horse and let the child work in a round pen or small enclosure. The child can make a mistake, and the results will not be a runaway animal and the child bouncing off the hard ground or pavement, or being dragged by the horse.

2. I personally like Western saddles and laid back older geldings (a fixed male). These horses are worth their weight in gold, as they can be a babysitter for a child or a great learning animal for an older adult while you lean to balance your body when you ride. If you purchased one of these horses for $3,000 (this is not an unreasonable price, depending on the economy) and used him to learn how to ride, the animal will keep its value when you want to move up to a different level.

3. After learning to ride Western style, if you like English riding, then switch, because you will have the balance to stay on the horse. Western saddles are for work, and they will help you stay in the saddle when making quick changes in direction. English saddles are for different purposes, and doing 360 spins or 90 degree turns are not its uses.

4. My Western saddle was made for me and my horse, and it is the best saddle I have ever ridden (custom saddles are not that expensive unless you go overboard with silver and other decorations). Outside of my personal saddle, my favorite is an Australian stock saddle, which are modified English saddles. They are very comfortable, and you can do any performance moves you can imagine.

5. You can participate in all kinds of events in the horse industry. Following are some of the activities, but it is not a complete list:

   - Racing (Thoroughbreds, Quarter Horses, Paints, and Arabian)

   - Reining (Quarter Horses, Paints, Arabians and mixed breeds)

   - Cutting (Quarter Horses, Paints, Arabians

   - Halter (almost all breeds)

- Western pleasure (most breeds)

- Trail rides for fun (any breed)

- Endurance riding (Arabians or Arab cross)

- Team penning and team sorting (Quarter Horses, Paints, Arabians—but best if they have been trained for cutting or reining before they get into the arena)

6. My favorite activities are reining and cutting. Reining is cheaper to do, because there are no cattle fees involved but both require the rider and the horse to become one. Also, the judging is fairest in these events. In important shows, they have five judges, and after the horse and rider perform they throw out the high score nd the low score. This makes your work less susceptible to politics.

7. I have a pet peeve when it comes to horses and kids or inexperienced riders.

   Many people go to sale barns and buy a horse that was built up to be the safest horse in the world. When the people get the horse home and ride it, they find out it is crazy and can't be handled. They discover that the horse had been drugged to calm it down. This is a big problem, particularly if someone falls off the horse and gets hurt.

8. Another problem with a new horse and an experienced rider is that horses are herd animals, and they would prefer not to be ridden. They can weigh from 900 to 1,300 pounds, and if they ever get the hint that they are in charge, and the rider doesn't know what he/she is doing, there is the potential for a disaster. Unknowing, inexperienced parents will saddle up (they probably don't know how to properly put on a saddle) a new horse and put an inexperienced child on the horse to go trail riding. This can be like putting the child on a bucking bull. There is a perfect solution for solving this problem:

   - Buy a sound horse from a reputable trainer who will prove to you that the horse is safe.

   - Pay for lessons until experience is achieved.

   - Never allow an inexperienced rider to ride in the open, on a trail or along a highway.

   - Start off with a small, round pen. Walking, jogging, and loping with a Western saddle is perfect to begin the process of riding. One needs to learn balance, and only experience will achieve that.

   - Riding bareback and English can teach or improve balance, but I like to get started with fun and safety, and then go to these other techniques.

- After becoming proficient in the round pen (40 to 50 feet across), it is time to move to a large pen or arena. By this time, the rider should be in charge of the horse, and the horse knows his place in life.

- You do not have to hurt the horse in any way to be in control. The horse respects the rider because he trusts the rider to care for him and not let him get hurt.

- I use the word "him" because the best horse for a new rider is a gelding, a horse that has been fixed so he is no longer a stallion. Mares (females) can be moody and are not as stable as most geldings.

Some females that are not good enough quality to be used for breeding are "fixed," and these can also be very stable and great for learning to ride.

9. DO NOT BUY A STALLION! Buying a stallion when you have little or no experience is a good way to get hurt—permanently. Even if you want to breed a really good mare, you don't need your stallion. There many good stallions available in every breed that you can use, which will cost you a lot less money and time than if you own a breeding stallion. There are three types of people who know stallions:

- The person who knows nothing about stallions, and the horse dominates them until they get hurt.

- Someone who thinks the way to handle a stallion is with fear and pain. They beat the horses into submission. I have seen trainers like this, and I was hoping the horse would win the battle. The stallion is usually not worth much after they have been mishandled.

- The third type recognizes that horses must be dominated but not through pain. They know there is a leader of the herd, and they put themselves in that position. The stallion recognizes that this person is a dominant "stallion," and they work hard and behave properly.

10. I love stallions. I love to work with them, and I love to ride them. But when I sense danger, I make them into geldings, because I don't want to get hurt by a 900 to 1,200 pound animal.

11. Horses are wonderful, but if they discover they can do what they want, then people or kids are in trouble. If you love horses, dominate them with love and positive training. You will have a great experience!

Soil

1. The soil is important if you want healthy horses. What was raised on your land before you took it over? Was it cropland? Pasture grassland? Were a lot of herbicides, pesticides, toxic lime and/or chemical fertilizers used on it? If any of these things were used (if the land was cropland, you can bet the farm that toxic chemicals of all kinds were used), you need to detoxify your land and your animals (in their feed).

2. Spreading humates is a very good way to detoxify the land.

3. Humates are somewhat like coal, and they are loaded with humid acid, folic acid and chelated minerals.

4. You also must consider what type of grass to grow. Many people want to restore native grasses that were present on the prairies before the settlers arrived. This is fine, but you must have lots of land that can be idle while the grasses become established. Even after restoration, you need a lot more land and grass than you have horses. Usually there is a local grass that does well that you already have that can be brought back. Check with local people to determine the best grass, and don't overstock or be prepared to feed hay until you get your grass established.

5. People's opinions are interesting. In our area, and all over the South, we have a grass called Bahia. Some people hate it and are obsessed with getting rid of it. It is actually a great grass if managed properly. It is also the last grass to turn brown and stop growing when winter approaches. The point is to investigate all grasses and go with what you can manage.

6. Soil is important. Texture has to do with clay, sand, rocky, or whatever. In the east, the soil and grasses can grow well, but the soil is worn out and the trace minerals are gone. The horses can eat themselves silly and still starve to death. In the West, the soils are thin, but there are a lot of limestone and other types of rocky soil. The horses don't have a lot to eat, but what they have is very nutritious.

7. Climate is also important, as some grasses need more water than others. Some areas can have two crops of grass per year. Here in the South, you can have summer grasses followed by winter rye, wheat, clover and/or oats.

8. When considering grass and pasture, what are you going to do to improve your land? The present system is to use chemicals to fertilize, and the theory is that plants

17

can't tell the difference between organics and chemicals. Only an idiot would advocate that man has a better way than the Maker.

9. Chemical fertilizers are mixed with industrial waste (1/3 to 2/3 per 50 lb bag), and it is spread on the soil. This will infuse nitrogen and make the grass grow with long stems and little leaves. This has been done mostly since World War II, and soils have not been supplemented with trace minerals in more than 70 years.

10. Industry has been forced to collect their pollutants and then dispose of them. If they can convince the Environmental Protection Agency (EPA) that their waste can be considered an element, it can be given to fertilizer companies to be mixed with fertilizers, and, unknown to farmers, it is spread on their land to poison the grasses, crops and animals. These chemicals tend to be heavy metals, lead, mercury, aluminum, arsenic, cadmium and many others. If they can't get these wastes into the fertilizer system, they have to dispose of them in toxic sites that cost a lot of money. It doesn't take a lot to see where they want to get rid of their wastes. The question you must ask is, "Do you want the risk of this stuff on your land and in your animals?"

11. Linus Pauling, Ph.D., winner of two Nobel prizes, once made the statement that all disease in people can be traced to the lack of trace minerals in the food. The same can be said about animals. Without the proper input, soils don't provide the essential nutrients for the health of people, horses, cows or other animals.

12. The soil in the United States had about 8% humus when it was first farmed. This reduced the heat buildup, absorbed rain water and had plenty of trace minerals and fertility. It also helped prevent flooding and droughts. Today, the humus is down to about 1% or less. With soil erosion taking soil, nutrients and chemicals to the Gulf of Mexico, I would suggest that the first thing you need to do is to restore humus to the soil.

13. There is very strong evidence that soil without humus may contribute to global warming.

14. DON'T use a mold board plow on your fields. This is the single biggest destroyer of farm land in the United States. It takes the aerobic material from the top and makes it into anaerobic material, and then it takes the anaerobic material and puts it on the top to make it aerobic material. This will not help your farm or your animals.

15. Restoring humus is not difficult but requires some money and/or labor and time.

16. The easiest way to add humus is to buy dry humates and put it out with a commercial spreader (one ton or more at a time) or smaller spreader (50 lb bags).

   I would put 100 to 200 lbs per acre per year (this is not only better but cheaper) for two to three years. This will detoxify previous chemicals, add trace minerals and make the land hold water instead of running off. And the worms will return to make the soil more porous and help restore beneficial bacteria.

17. There are many other ways to improve the soil and it depends on your pocketbook to determine w hat you will do for the improvement. I like sprays for a number of reasons - less work and less money. Liquid molasses is one of the cheapest ways to start improving your land.

18. To use liquids, you need a sprayer. They are not overly expensive and can sometimes be rented, but be careful. If herbicides and pesticides have been used in the sprayer, don't use it. Even a tiny amount is toxic. Farmers have a very high rate of cancer caused by tiny amounts of chemicals.

19. Molasses is very good way to start restoring your land and the health of your horses. You can get molasses from the feed store under various names. In our area, it is called Cat-A-Lac, and it is used as a feed in the winter. For the life of me, I haven't figured out why you would want to feed this stuff instead of good hay. It's probably because they don't have good hay (all the chemicals and "stuff"). This molasses is about a dollar a gallon, and if that is the only thing I could afford, then I would put three to four gallons per acre.

20. Water is important in this process. If you don't have a well (clean water without chlorine), then put water in the tank and let it set, with the lid off, for two days to allow the volatile chemicals to pass into the air.

21. Molasses has two qualities that I like (besides the price). It has a lot of trace minerals, and the sugar content feeds the microbes in the soil until the soil is in balance and stabilized, creating soil fertility.

22. If you watch too much TV, you will get the idea that bacteria are all bad and we want to kill them. This is not true. In fact, there are beneficial bacteria and bad bacteria. If you have a good immune system, checks and balances between the bacteria lead to good health. The soil is the same. Bacteria need food and molasses is a great food for them.

23. You are bound to have a debate at some point with your "good ole boy" neighbors that you need to add lime to your soil. This is not true. If you improve your soil with my suggestions, you will never need lime; the pH will become stabilized close to neutral (slightly alkaline 7.2) in a few years.

24. A warning should you decide to use lime: Lime has various components, and most feed stores have no idea of this fact. If you ask them to find out what is in their lime, you will get various blank looks — something like a door knob. They also don't want to find out due to the effort involved. I get various responses, but the most common is, "It's okay Doc. I have been using this lime all my life, and it is okay. In fact, my daddy used this lime." This may be all well and good, but I want to know what my soil is getting. Lime can vary in calcium content and other chemicals, not to mention that toxic wastes have been mixed in with lime to get rid of it just as in fertilizers.

25. If you can't find out what is in a product, you don't need it.

26. Another ingredient I like to use to help the soil are liquid humates. Liquid humates are not as good as dry humates, but they are inexpensive, they detoxify the water and the soil and they help to add trace minerals to the soil.

27. There have been many studies done on humates. National Institute of Health (NIH) studies have found that one of its benefits is to depress or reduce the effects of viruses on our immune system. This applies to colds, flu and even AIDS. Humates as supplements can be found on my website for people, cows and horses (www.drbobthehealthbuilder.com).

28. My favorite soil additive is seawater. Don't get all worked up that salt will kill your plants, because it will not. In fact, if you don't have salt (NaCl), the other trace minerals will not be absorbed into the plants (there are studies to prove this). On my website (www.drbobthehealthbuilder.com), I carry a seawater from Australia with most of the salt removed.

29. Where does the seawater come from? Years ago, a surgeon, Dr. Murray, became worried that he was seeing more and more cancer in people, with an increase in surgery. He developed an interest in the sea and discovered that all seawater was the same. He also found out that fish and mammals from the ocean never had cancer, whereas people and freshwater fish frequently had cancer. He got the idea to use what was then called sea solids to put on farm land. Sea solids had trace minerals and were therefore replacing trace minerals that had been "mined" from the farm land.

30. Today, we use ocean water because unlike sea solids it has 92 trace minerals, amino acids, enzymes and beneficial bacteria. Ocean water is a complete supplement for growing plants.

31. Another very good product to use is compost. This is a lot of work, but you can take manure, leaves, grass, saw dust, tree trimmings, old hay or anything organic, and put it into a pile to rot (putting molasses or anything sugary into the pile is great). Depending on weather and other factors, this will reduce down by at least one half. After the compost is finished, you can spread it on your pastures, and it will work miracles.

32. Another way to get the benefits of compost without all the work is to make the compost and then soak it in a container of water. After the tea brews for a day or two, add molasses and let it work. After about one week, aerate the liquid to make beneficial fungus, along with the bacteria, and then put the liquid on the soil. This is a foliar feed for the plants. After it rains, the mixture is taken into the root zone. After you put this spray out, always wait for it to rain before you bale hay.

33. I use the humates and ocean water twice a year and the molasses and aerated compost tea at least foour times a year (and sometimes five or six times a year).

Breeding

1. Breeding (delivery or birthing) is a whole other life for you and the horse. If you let them alone, they do better, but you still need to watch them in case they have a problem with delivery. I don't know how many babies we had, but we never had a complication. If you want real problems, induce the mares, and you will have nightmares for years to come.

2. I am a great believer in letting well enough alone, meaning let the mare take care of the baby while you stand back and admire and keep your hands to yourself most of the time. You don't need special supplements if you are feeding the mare quality hay, as I have written (I have a new book, *Intelligent Ramblings of a Healthy Farmer*). Regular supplements like humates and diatomaceous earth are fine, but you don't need special supplements for pregnant mares.

3. You do need to handle the babies to get them accustomed to people. Gather them up in your arms and gently restrain them while talking to them. Get them and their mother in a small confined area several times a week, and corner the babies and start brushing them and talking to them. Otherwise, let them out into a pasture to run and play to stretch their joints and muscles. The babies drive their mothers' nuts for the first few days with their running, but it is good exercise for the mares and babies.

4. There is nothing worse than confinement for horses—mares and foals. When they are in training you don't have a choice, but otherwise get them in a pasture or don't breed them.

5. Should *you* breed horses? The answer to that is probably NO.

6. Horses are like dogs. People think horses are cute and they are going to make money breeding them. The truth is, most people don't make money. I am not saying you can't make money; it is just that most people don't take time to learn how to breed animals that someone wants to buy.

7. Where do unwanted dogs end up? They end up at the animal shelter and have to be put to sleep. Where do the unwanted horses end up? They go to sale barns, where they are purchased and taken to slaughter plants and sold to the European countries for meat. You may find this disgusting, but it is real life. The bottom line is that 10% to 20% of horses end up as food each year.

8. This has changed due to federal laws, so some horse get eaten because they are shipped to Mexico or Canada. Some are turned loose by their owners who can't afford them during an economic downturn. And some starve to death in fields without grass. All sad but true.

9. Breeding horses is an art and a subject all its own, but let me make some suggestions: Buy a horse or two and *you* take care of them — not an employee.

10. Learn their habits and needs. Handle them, feed them, worm them and RIDE them.

11. If you like halter classes go for it, but do it on a local level, because if you take on the big boys they will out-money and outlast you. If you like Western, try reining, cutting or Western pleasure. If you like English, try dressage, jumping, park or competing in buggy classes. There are many types of activities to do with horses, but do them before you start breeding. When you find your passion, go with it, but make sure there is a need for your "product" so your animals don't end up as steak in France.

12. When you decide to breed, buy the best mare you can afford, and breed her to the best stallion you can afford, but do not breed her just because the stallion is close by or because he is cheap.

Farm Equipment

1. I have not mentioned transportation, but it is essential. Other than on your farm or neighborhood riding, you will need to move your horse from point A to point B. It is best to have a truck. Most cars today are not big enough to haul a trailer of any kind. I prefer a stock trailer instead of a one- or two-horse trailer. Horses like the extra room, and they will almost always load better in stock trailers. Once they learn to load and travel, most will like to travel. With our stallion, you had better get out of his way when loading, because he loves it, and he is ready to be a road warrior whenever we are ready to go. Once the horse learns to load and travel, you can get them into a horse trailer, whether it is for one or six.

2. Our horses almost never ate when traveling, and they were never interested in water, but then we never traveled more than six to eight hours. Cross-country riding is different, and water, hay and occasional exercise are important.

3. When we sold or bought a horse from other parts of the country, it was easier and cheaper to hire a trucking company that specializes in transporting horses over long distances

4. I do not believe in feeding grain or pellets to horses as they travel, because they need extra water with these feeds.

5. If you can afford to buy a tractor, get a new one that is easier to finance than used ones. If you are running your farm as a business, everything works better, including loans and employees. If money is a problem, you can sometimes find a used tractor in good shape, but as with a used car, you can also buy a worn out lemon. Find someone knowledgeable about tractors, and let them look before you lay out any hard-earned cash or get a loan.

6. Tractors come in all kinds of sizes for every job you can imagine. I have had five tractors over the years. I had two small ones that were very frustrating for more than seven acres, because it took too long to accomplish anything. We had a 40 horsepower tractor, and it worked well for 20 years, taking care of our needs. But when I started doing other peoples' hay fields with organic fertilizers, I needed a bigger tractor to carry a 200-gallon spray rig. I got a 50 horsepower tractor that worked well, but due to the larger size and a terrible seat, I bounced until I thought my insides were going to do flip-flops. I have since changed to a 65 horsepower tractor, which is comfortable, and I don't bounce thanks to the air shock control in the seat. We have 51 acres, and the 65 horses works well. If you have a lot more acreage, you should consider an even bigger tractor.

7. In some parts of the United States, they still use gasoline tractors, but for the most part you will do better with diesel, and you will find more mechanics to work on them if a need arises.

8. One of the mistakes I made on the old tractor was not having a frontend loader, which is better than sliced bread. I can't tell you how many things I do with the loader to prevent backbreaking work and for convenience.

9. When considering a tractor, you also must consider how you will feed your horses. It may take several years before you can use nothing but pasture. Most horse hay is in squares, but having a bucket can make it easier. We also use round bales that weigh from 1,200 lbs to 2,000 lbs (1 ton). You need a tractor for these.

Equine Health

1. We haven't mentioned feet, but it is an important issue. Just like with people, if the shoes don't fit, a horse will walk funny, its feet will get sore and it won't move properly.

2. Most horse farriers are idiots and will mess your animals up to the point that they have serious problems. There *are* good farriers though; find them and pay their fees. They are worth it.

3. Some people take their horses' shoes off in the winter, but I find it takes too long to get them back in shape in the spring.

    It doesn't cost that much extra to keep them in shape.

4. Mares and other horses you are not riding don't usually need shoes, but you will need to trim them every six to seven weeks to prevent any lameness (trouble walking or moving).

5. Horse health and feet will be influenced by their feed. I have a deal with my hay guy. I fertilize his field organically, and he gives me healthy hay. If you put trace minerals on the pasture and hay meadows, you will not need supplements. I know this is hard to believe, but it is true. If you can't get good hay, the best supplement is humates, because of the trace minerals and detoxification properties.

6. With organic fertilizers, you can spray any time; however, I like to do it after the plants are up, so the leaves absorb some of the nutrients, and the rest is taken under the surface to the roots after the first rain.

7. I haven't mentioned veterinarians, but they are important. For the most part, they are like medical doctors. They have been educated in land grant colleges, and their education has been controlled by drug and chemical companies. I have two vets that I use, and they are willing to work with me on my organic program. Be up front with them and offer them information. It may not change them with their other clients, but it will help you.

8. The size of your property and the number of animals has everything to do with your horses ending up with parasites (worms). In lots where animals stand next to each other for weeks, sharing food and water and lying or standing in each other's excrement, there are bound to be health issues. In the chemical world, they spray

these animals' backs with various chemicals, including organophosphates and other toxic chemicals.

There is now evidence that mad cow disease was caused by chemicals instead of feeding animal parts to cows. These types of chemicals are not necessary. Don't overload fields with too many horses, and use natural things for "worming." We use diatomaceous earth (DE). I mentioned before that this is good for the land and the animals, but it is also great for worming, and despite what vets and county agents might say, it works. (Texas A&M University did a study on this product with goats, and it worked well, but they took it off their website because the chemical boys that pay their graduate program don't want that type of information out to consumers.)

Financial Concerns

1. I have not mentioned money because the cost of land varies all over the United States, but there are some things you need to know. Farming and ranching are businesses, if you run them that way. Unless you are going to do this for fun—and there is no tax relief for fun—the government recognizes that it takes time to build a business, and they help you accomplish it with tax deductions against ordinary income, making it possible to get started.

2. One type of deduction is from tractors. When you buy a new tractor, you get investment tax credits that take a lot of money off your taxes immediately. The balance comes off over a period of time. When you buy a used tractor, there is no investment tax credit, but you do get to write off the cost of the tractor over a set period of time.

3. Horses have a different depreciation schedule than tractors.

4. Hay, feed and other supplies are written off immediately; there is no depreciation for this kind of expense.

5. The best advice on tax matters is to consult with a good CPA. They will save you more money than you pay them, and, besides, their expense is also a tax write-off. Be careful choosing a CPA, as not all of them know about farming and ranching. Some will lie and tell you they know something when they don't, and they will not research the needed materials. My CPA doesn't know beans about horses, but he's excellent because he researches everything. If he doesn't know something, he asks me and then digs up more info. I would recommend him to anyone if I am asked.

6. Property taxes are important to know about. The agricultural exemption is very important, and you need to know about your area—state or county. Property taxes vary from place to place. There is a big difference between having an ag exemption and not having it. We recently bought 11 acres next to our farm, and the county made a mistake. The difference between not having it was $1,100 vs. $11. I would never cheat, but you need to find the standards for your area. Five acres will require some number of animals to keep the exemption.

7. Some counties do not allow horses as an exemption, even if the people are making money.

8. The idea of raising, training or selling horses is to make money and save taxes. The way to make money in the horse business is complicated, but most people do not

make money breeding and selling the million dollar horse. Although this can be done, and you should strive for this, the surest way to make money is to buy the best piece of land that you can afford in an area where there is growth of housing, people and jobs. Buy the best horse you can afford, usually a mare, and breed her to the best stallion you can find, and over a period of years keep your fillies, show your colts and fillies, and sell some to get cash flow.

After years in the business, you hope you can break even in the horse business as your land appreciates. If you have been doing a great job, your horses should be worth a great deal of money when you want to retire. Sell the horses for a profit, then sell the land for a profit, and then take your proceeds from the sale. Then retire, having had fun in the horse business. Along the way, if you are good in the horse business and in showing, you might become a judge and add extra income to your retirement by judging shows.

Questions?

Please write me at drbobcowblog@gmail.com if you have any questions or comments, and I will get back with you as soon possible.

Dr. Robert D. Bard, OD, FAAO, ONS (Dr. Bob)

Resources

The Mule Fence
www.geotekinc.com

Humate Supplement
Humates FP
www.drbobthehealthbuilder.com

Horse breeds
www.maroon.com

Ocean water for fertilizer
Total Ocean Nutrition - Trace Minerals
www.drbobthehealthbuilder.com

For Soil and Farm Animals
Monthly newspaper on organics
www.acresusa.com (also has a large reference library)

Newspaper on grass farming
www.stockmangrassfarmer.com (addresses chemicals and organics in the U.S. and from around the world)

Seeds of Deception by Jeffrey Smith
www.seedsofdeception.com (great information on genetically modified foods)

My health resource site
www.drbobthehealthbuilder.com

Podcast
www.drbobthehealthbuilder.podcast.com

Weekly newsletter
www.wealthyhealthywise.net

new book *Eat Healthy, Feel Better, Live Longer* and *Dr Bob's 100 Year Old Recipes*
www.eathealthyU.com

Special product for preventing hangovers after an evening of too much drinking
www.pardonyourhang over.com